WHAT MAKES
SPORTS GEAR
SAFER?

KEVIN KURTZ

LERNER PUBLICATIONS ◆ **MINNEAPOLIS**

TO ADAM AND NOAH

Content Consultant: Patrick Drane, Assistant Director, Baseball Research Center, University of Massachusetts Lowell

Lerner Publications Company
A division of Lerner Publishing Group, Inc.
241 First Avenue North
Minneapolis, MN 55401 USA

For reading levels and more information, look up this title at www.lernerbooks.com.

Main body text set in Caecilia Com 55 Regular 11/16
Typeface provided by Linotype AG.

Library of Congress Cataloging-in-Publication Data

Kurtz, Kevin, author.
    What makes sports gear safer? / Kevin Kurtz.
      pages cm. — (Engineering keeps us safe)
    Summary: "This book uses engineering, science, and common sense to examine the clothing and sports equipment technology we have in place to keep us safe."—Provided by the publisher.
    Audience: Ages 9–12.
    Audience: Grades 4 to 6.
    Includes bibliographical references and index.
    ISBN 978-1-4677-7915-9 (lib : alk. paper) — ISBN 978-1-4677-8650-8 (EB pdf)
    1. Sports—Safety measures—Juvenile literature. 2. Sporting goods—Juvenile literature. 3. Sports—Technological innovations—Juvenile literature. I. Title.
GV344.K87 2015
796.028'4—dc23
                                       2014041984

Manufactured in the United States of America
1 – VP – 7/15/15

CONTENTS

PLAY IT SAFE!

If you follow sports, you've probably heard about dramatic sports-related injuries in the news. And it's no surprise that these stories make headlines. After all, tales about fiery NASCAR crashes and career-ending concussions sell papers. They get people to tune into news broadcasts and click links to online articles.

Sports injuries are nothing to take lightly. Athletes suffer from injuries every day. Yet truly devastating sports-related injuries really aren't as common as we are led to think. Most people play sports without ever experiencing a serious injury. One big reason for this is sports gear. Sports gear has two purposes. It improves the performance of athletes, helping them run faster, jump higher, and hit balls farther. And it also helps athletes stay safe.

Sports engineers design sports gear. They study what causes sports injuries. Then they think about how to prevent these injuries. Engineers use physics, chemistry, and new technologies to design the best gear. Their work allows everyone to be safer while playing sports.

So the next time you step up to bat in a baseball game or lace up a pair of hockey skates, remember your protective gear. Engineers have worked hard to design sports equipment to keep you safe. Be sure to wear all that special equipment they designed and follow your coach's advice about how to play smart and prevent injuries. If you do so, you'll be playing it safe and playing to win!

Pads and headgear protect hockey players on the ice.

WHY HELMETS ARE HARD

A bicyclist is riding down the road. She does not see a small rock in front of her. When her front tire hits the rock, she flies over the handlebars. Her head hits the ground. Yet when she stands up, she does not have any scratches or bruises on her head. That is because she was wearing her bicycle helmet!

Sports helmets are designed to help protect the head from impact injuries. An impact injury is what happens when your body runs into another object. When that bicyclist hit the ground, her forward motion suddenly stopped. Energy cannot disappear, so some of that energy bounced back into her head. The energy from an impact creates a powerful force. It can cause pain and injury. Helmets can reduce the impact energy reaching the head.

Most helmets have a hard outer shell and a rounded shape. This shape helps spread out the energy of the impact. If a ball hits a player's bare head, all the energy from the ball flows into one spot on the head. If a ball hits a helmet, the energy spreads out over a larger surface area of the helmet.

Each spot gets a little bit of the energy instead of one spot getting all of it. By spreading out the energy, helmets make serious injuries much less likely.

The hard plastic and the rounded shape of bicycle helmets help spread out the energy from an impact.

Remember to always wear your bicycle helmet when riding your bike.

STRONG BUT LIGHTWEIGHT

Most major-league pitchers throw baseballs at a speed of more than 90 miles (145 kilometers) per hour. Sometimes wild pitches hit a batter in the head. Batters wear helmets to protect themselves.

A batting helmet needs to be strong but light. A heavy helmet would make it harder for the batter to move quickly. Batting helmets used to be made out of simple plastic. Plastic is lightweight, but it's not very strong. Most plastic helmets are designed to protect batters from pitches 55 miles (89 km) per hour. Pitches can exceed 100 miles (161 km) per hour, so these are not the best helmets for baseball players.

Some batting helmets are now made of carbon-fiber materials. Carbon-fiber helmets help protect batters' heads from pitches that travel faster than 100 miles (161 km) per hour. And these helmets are almost as lightweight as plastic helmets.

Carbon-fiber helmets are lightweight and strong because they are made out of the element carbon. Carbon can form bonds that make crystals. Carbon crystals do not contain many atoms. This makes the carbon crystals lightweight.

Professional baseball helmets are made from sheets of carbon-fiber material.

When carbon atoms bond together, they can be very hard to break apart. This strong bond makes the carbon fiber very strong. Carbon fibers are stronger than steel! The carbon crystals can be woven together to make sheets of carbon. The sheets are then molded and coated with plastic to make the outer shell of the helmet.

Professional baseball players wear carbon-fiber helmets for protection.

WHY HELMETS ARE SOFT INSIDE

Helmets have crushable pads inside. Good helmet pads are soft and comfortable. They require a lot of energy to crush them. The pads need special material in them to absorb impact energy. Football players sometimes run headfirst into each other, even though they should not do this. Some of the impact energy travels through the outer shell of their helmets. That energy immediately hits and crushes the pads. Because the impact energy is used to shrink the pads, less of it reaches the athlete's head. The pads will then slowly stretch back to normal size. This releases the energy without hurting the player.

Football helmets often have pads made of polypropylene or vinyl nitrile foam. Polypropylene and vinyl nitrile are types of polymers. They can be dense, flexible, and hard to break. This makes them great for football helmets. Football players hit their heads all the time. Polypropylene and vinyl nitrile foam pads keep working after many hits.

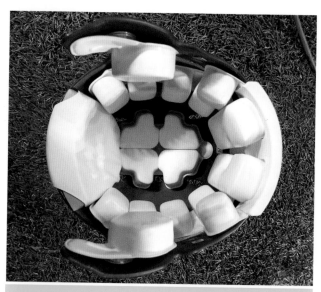

A football helmet has lots of padding inside (above). Helmets are essential safety gear in football (right).

AN AIR BAG FOR YOUR HEAD

A new bicycle helmet available in Europe works like a car air bag. The bicyclist wears the helmet as a collar around the neck. Electronic sensors in the collar pay attention to how the rider is moving. If the bicyclist flies over the handlebars, the sensors act as though a crash is about to happen. The sensors trigger the air bag helmet to inflate out of the collar. In less than a second, helium fills the helmet. The helmet grows twice as big as a normal helmet. When the helmet hits the ground, the impact energy squeezes the helium together. This keeps the energy from reaching the head.

HELMETS ARE NOT PERFECT

Helmets are good at stopping some head injuries. But they are not good at stopping concussions.

The brain is surrounded by liquid in the skull. This liquid usually cushions the brain from regular jolts. An athlete gets a concussion when his head hits something with so much force that his brain is pushed against his skull. A helmet cannot stop the brain from doing this. Many doctors and scientists doubt a helmet will ever keep players safe from concussions.

Often it's hard to tell when a player has a concussion. If a player with a concussion keeps playing, she can hurt herself even more. Sports engineers have developed electronic motion sensors to help with this problem.

Some of these sensors are inside helmet pads. Each sensor measures how much the pad crushes around it when a player gets hit. A big impact makes the padding crush a lot. That information tells the sensor that a concussion is likely.

Other sensors are in mouth guards. A mouth guard sensor is held tight by the athlete's teeth. The sensor measures how fast the skull speeds up and stops. It uses this information to predict whether a player has a concussion.

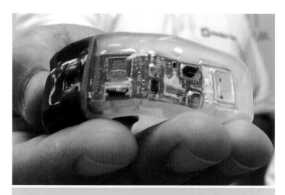

Sensors inside mouth guards can detect possible concussions.

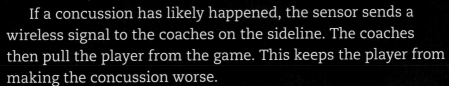

If a concussion has likely happened, the sensor sends a wireless signal to the coaches on the sideline. The coaches then pull the player from the game. This keeps the player from making the concussion worse.

But concussion sensors are not perfect. They don't catch all concussions because some players may get a concussion from a light impact or even a hit to the chest. The sensors are not programmed to detect these. But as engineers keep learning more, they will be able to build better sensors.

A doctor needs to check any player suspected of receiving a concussion.

SMART PADS

Athletes in some sports wear pads to protect their knees and shins. Some new pads in soccer, mountain biking, and other sports use "smart" padding. This padding stays soft when the athlete is moving. When something hits the pad, the padding immediately hardens. When the smart pad turns solid, the hard pad spreads the impact energy over a larger area of the body. Once the impact is over, the padding softens again.

Smart pads work like oobleck. If you have ever mixed cornstarch and water together, then you have made oobleck. When oobleck is in a bowl, it acts like a liquid. When oobleck is squeezed, it immediately feels hard like a solid.

Smart pads and oobleck are non-Newtonian fluids. A non-Newtonian fluid stays soft like a liquid until it feels pressure from an impact or squeezing. Then the fluid immediately turns into a hard solid.

Scientists are still trying to figure out why this happens. One theory is the rapid change in pressure makes all the fluid particles suddenly move very quickly. This basically causes a traffic jam. Then the particles cannot move at all. This makes them act like a solid. They stay a solid until the pressure stops.

Kids play with oobleck, which hardens and softens as smart pads do.

Soccer players rely on pads to protect their shins.

KEEPING A BOTTLE FROM BREAKING

Smart padding is used in soccer shin guards. To show how they work, a shin guard manufacturer wrapped a smart shin guard around a glass bottle. He then dropped a bowling ball on the bottle. When the bowling ball hit the shin guard, the padding immediately hardened and the bottle didn't break.

STAYING SAFE IN A DANGEROUS SPOT

Baseball and softball catchers have one of the most dangerous jobs in sports. Catchers often get hit hard by balls, bats, and runners. Catchers are covered from head to toe in protective sports gear.

A catcher's hand takes a lot of abuse. Pitches can strike the hand at speeds of more than 90 miles (145 km) per hour. The pitches also spin at incredible speeds. A curveball may spin around thirty times every second. The spin adds even more energy to the impact of the ball on the catcher's hand.

Catchers' mitts have padding to absorb impact. Some mitts are also covered with dimples. The dimples slow down the spin of a ball. These tiny bumps create friction when the ball hits the glove. The friction quickly slows the ball's spin and decreases the ball's energy.

Catchers can also be hit in the chest by balls, bats, and runners. They wear chest protectors to absorb these blows. Some early chest protectors were made of leather that was stuffed with wool. Modern chest protectors are padded with high-tech materials, such as thermoplastic polyurethane. This type of padding is designed to

Thermoplastic polyurethane pebbles are used to make high-tech baseball catchers' pads.

absorb as much energy as possible. It is lightweight because it is not very dense. This makes modern chest protectors weigh half as much as those used one hundred years ago. And they are more effective.

Baseball catchers use padded mitts and chest protectors to protect themselves from the impact of balls, bats, and runners.

RUNNING ON AIR

Running can cause injuries. A runner's feet are constantly slamming on the ground. The energy from these impacts is carried through the feet up to the knees. Though our bodies are built to handle the impact of running, running injuries can still happen. Good running shoes are designed to help cushion feet and legs.

Since 1979, many running shoes have been cushioned with air. The air is contained in little pads between the shoe's sole and the runner's foot. When the runner's foot hits the ground, the impact energy enters the pad. It causes the air to squeeze together, which absorbs the energy so it does not reach the foot. When the foot lifts, the air spreads out again. It is then ready to absorb the next impact.

RUNNING ON BLADES

A shoe design that was released in 2013 doesn't look like any other shoe. It has sixteen plastic blades sticking out of each sole. The runner runs on the blades. They help protect the runner from the impact of running.

As the runner's feet hit the ground, the impact energy makes each blade squish like a spring. This reduces the energy reaching the foot. These blades also help the runner go faster. When she lifts her foot, the blades release their energy. The energy then strikes the ground and pushes the runner forward.

Air cushions have many other advantages. Air cushions last longer than foam cushions , which have been used in the past. Foam pads in athletic shoes fall apart after a while. Air does not break down. This keeps runners safer longer. Air is also really lightweight. Athletes like this because air pads make the shoe lighter and don't weigh the runners down.

Cushioned running shoes help keep athletes' feet and knees healthy.

A SNEAKER LIKE A SUSPENSION BRIDGE

Athletes sometimes get injured by spraining their ankles. A sprain happens when the ankle rolls in the wrong direction and a ligament is torn.

The high-top sneaker is designed to support ankles. This sneaker has a higher top than other athletic shoes. High-tops wrap material around an athlete's ankles to hold them in place. The ankles are then less likely to roll and sprain.

Basketball players have worn high-top sneakers for about one hundred years. But in 2008, a low-top sneaker that supports the ankle was released. These low-top sneakers use technology that was inspired by suspension bridges.

Suspension bridges have towers. Supporting cables stretch horizontally to each tower. Vertical cables connect the supporting cables to the bridge deck. The low-top sneakers have fibers that act like cables on a suspension bridge. The shoe wraps thin fibers around the places in the foot that need support. The fibers make a web pattern around the foot. The fibers grip the foot like a sock and provide support.

fibers that create tension and grip the foot

SNEAKER SUSPENSION

These sneaker fibers are made of Vectran. Vectran is a polyester material spun from liquid crystals. Vectran fibers are thinner than a human hair and five times stronger than steel. The fibers are strong enough to act like the foot's tendons. They support the foot so the ankle is less likely to roll.

Sports engineers use the science behind suspension bridges to design shoes.

AVALANCHE SAFETY

Some skiers and snowboarders prefer backcountry skiing and snowboarding to swooshing down groomed slopes. They hike up a mountain with their gear. Then they ride down fresh snow that no one else has touched yet. This can be a great experience. But these backcountry athletes are at risk of being buried by an avalanche.

These athletes wear backpacks with avalanche air bags. When they see an avalanche forming around them, they push a button or pull a rip cord on the backpack. A compressed air tank blows air into the air bag. The air bag inflates behind or on the sides of the athlete in a couple of seconds.

A concept called particle size segregation is what helps an air bag protect the athlete. If you have ever opened a can of mixed nuts, you may have noticed the biggest nuts are at the top. This is because of particle size segregation. When many different-sized objects are shaken, the biggest objects rise to the top.

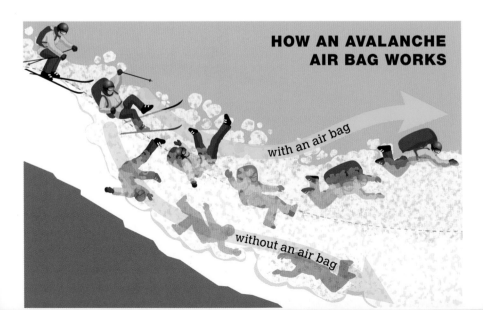

HOW AN AVALANCHE AIR BAG WORKS

with an air bag

without an air bag

The air bag turns the athlete into the biggest object in the avalanche. As the avalanche rolls, the smaller chunks of snow sort to the bottom. The athlete sorts to the top. The bag keeps her from being buried deep in the snow. This will make it easier for rescuers to uncover her.

If a backcountry skier gets caught in an avalanche, an air bag could save his life.

A DIGITAL SIGNAL FOR HELP

Many backcountry skiers carry avalanche beacons. The beacon produces a radio signal that can travel through snow. Rescuers carry a receiver that picks up the signal. The digital receivers calculate the distance and the direction to the buried skier. The rescuer can then quickly find the buried skier and dig her out.

SAFETY FOR ROCK CLIMBERS

A woman is climbing a steep cliff. Her hand reaches and grips a rock, but the rock breaks loose and she falls. She is tied to another climber for safety. The other climber is not strong enough to stop a 130-pound (59-kilogram) woman from falling. Yet the falling climber is safely stopped.

She was saved by a belay system. This connects two climbers by a rope. One end of the rope is tied to a harness on the lead climber. The other end of the rope runs through a belay device attached to the person below. The person below is called the belayer. The belayer stays in one place to be ready if the climber falls. His belay device creates friction on the rope. Friction stops the climber from falling.

Friction occurs when a moving object rubs against another object. Say you push a friend who is sitting on a sled on snowy ground. He moves quickly in the sled but then stops. Friction slows and eventually stops the sled because the sled runs out of energy.

A belay device forces the rope to make a tight loop and touch metal in three places. The end of the rope is held in the

A climber's rope runs through an anchor, which is designed to hold the climber's weight if she falls.

belayer's hand. If the climber falls, the belayer pulls the rope tight. His hand creates friction on the rope. The metal in the belay device increases the friction. There is then so much friction on the rope that it locks up. The belayer barely used any of his own strength and energy to stop the falling climber. The friction of the belay device did all the work for him.

Even a skilled climber falls occasionally, making a belay system essential.

A SMOOTH RIDE ON A BUMPY TRAIL

A mountain biker needs a good mountain bike to be safe. A mountain biker rides over rocks and branches at high speeds. The bike needs to absorb the shock of every bump. If it doesn't, the biker will feel those impacts in the body.

A mountain bike's suspension system is designed to absorb the shock of riding. Most of the shock absorption happens in the fork. The fork is attached above the front tire and to the axle, or the bar the wheel turns on. The fork contains a spring and dampers that absorb impact energy. The spring can be metal coils or compressed air. Impact energy squeezes the spring or the air. This keeps the energy from hitting the rider all at once.

MEET A MOUNTAIN BIKE ENGINEER

David Weagle is a mountain bike engineer. As a kid, David loved fast sports and building things. His job combines both these loves. He has designed new mountain bike suspension systems such as dw-link and Split Pivot. The dw-link system reduces how much a biker bobs up and down while riding. Split Pivot creates a smoother ride by separating the acceleration forces from the braking forces on the rear wheel of a bike.

Weagle's ideas start with riding his bike. He imagines ways to improve the riding experience. He may spend a year on a computer working out the physics for a new idea. The design on the computer is then used to make a model. The model is tested on the trails. If it passes all its tests, it is manufactured and sold in stores.

When the spring releases the energy, the rider does not bounce up and down. This is because the dampers use the energy released by the spring. The energy forces oil through a small hole in each damper. As the oil squeezes through the hole, work is being performed. Because the energy is lost to the work completed, it does not reach the rider.

Thanks to a mountain bike's suspension system, a biker can ride over rocks without too much jarring.

THE FUTURE OF SAFE SPORTS GEAR

The sports gear we use fits thousands of people the same way. But every person is different. Sports gear may work well for one person. But it may not work at all for a person with a different body type.

In the future, we likely won't have this problem. Sports gear may be made from 3-D printers to fit each person perfectly. This gear will be much better at keeping you safe.

More sports gear will also contain electronic sensors. These sensors will record data about what happens to your body while playing sports. This data can then be used to make even better sports gear for you.

Sports may never be completely injury-free. But future sports gear will likely make athletes even safer. This will allow all of us to keep playing our favorite sports.

A company has started 3-D printing soles of athletic shoes that are customized to athletes' feet and movement and that improve performance.

GLOSSARY

avalanche: a large amount of snow or ice that suddenly falls down the side of a mountain

carbon fibers: strong, lightweight material used in protective gear

concussion: a serious injury caused by the brain hitting the skull inside the head

damper: a device that absorbs impact energy and spreads it out by squeezing oil through a small hole

dense: having parts that are close together so the material is compact

friction: a force that happens when two objects rub against each other, which slows down the speed of the moving object

impact injury: an injury caused when a person collides with an object. Impact injuries include bruises, broken bones, sprains, and concussions.

sensor: an electronic device that can measure and record what is going on around it. A sensor's data can often be shared with a computer.

surface area: a measurement of the amount of space covering an object

SELECTED BIBLIOGRAPHY

Bramson, Kate. "R.I. Firm's High-Tech Shin Guards Give Some International Soccer Players a Leg Up." *Providence Journal.* July 1, 2014. http://www. providencejournal.com/breaking-news/content/20140701-r.i.-firms-high -tech-shin-guards-give-some-international-soccer-players-a-leg-up.ece.

Cardona, Melissa. *The Sneaker Book: 50 Years of Sports Shoe Design.* Atglen, PA: Schiffer, 2005.

Fainaru-Wada, Mark, and Steve Fainaru. *League of Denial: The NFL, Concussions, and the Battle for Truth.* New York: Crown Archetype, 2013.

Osborne, Ben, ed. *Slam Kicks: Basketball Sneakers That Changed the Game.* New York: Universe, 2014.

Shyr, Luna. "NFL Looks to Helmet Technology to Combat Concussions." *National Geographic,* February 1, 2013. http://news.nationalgeographic.com /news/2013/13/130202-football-concussions-nfl-super-bowl-safety-head -injuries-health/.

Vizard, Frank, ed. *Why a Curveball Curves: The Incredible Science of Sports.* New York: Hearst, 2008.

LERNER

SOURCE

Expand learning beyond the printed book. Download free, complementary educational resources for this book from our website, www.lerneresource.com.

FURTHER INFORMATION

Design Squad Nation
http://pbskids.org/designsquad
This website gives you lots of cool engineering and design activities to try.

Love, Carrie, Penny Smith, and Margaret Parrish, eds. *How Things Work Encyclopedia*. New York: DK, 2010. Learn some of the science behind engineering.

Savage, Jeff. *Deadly Hard-Hitting Sports*. Minneapolis: Lerner Publications, 2013. Learn more about the risks taken by athletes who do extreme sports.

Sports Illustrated Kids
http://www.sikids.com
The website for *Sports Illustrated Kids* magazine will keep you up to date on the latest news about sports and sports gear.

Sports Illustrated Kids. Big Book of Why Sports Edition. New York: Time Home Entertainment, 2012. This book of fun facts will teach you all about sports.

Time for Kids. Big Book of Why: Amazing Sports and Science. New York: Time Home Entertainment, 2014. If you're looking for more sports facts, you'll find them in this intriguing volume.

INDEX

PHOTO ACKNOWLEDGMENTS

The images in this book are used with the permission of: © iStockphoto.com/ CynthiaAnnF, p. 1; © NY Daily News/Getty Images, p. 5 (background); © Chuck Myers/MCT/Getty Images, p. 5 (inset); © iStockphoto.com/Floortje, p. 6; © Jacek Chabraszewski/Dreamstime.com, pp. 6–7; © GraficallyMinded/Alamy, p. 8; © Mitchell Leff/Getty Images, p. 9; © Tom Szczerbowski/Getty Images, p. 10; © Stephen M. Dowell/Getty Images, p. 11; Hovding/Splash News/Newscom, p. 11 (inset); Amanda Harnocz/Northeast Ohio Media Group/The Plain Dealer/ Landov, p. 12; AP Photo/The LaPorte Herald-Argus, Bob Wellinski, p. 13; AP Photo/The Herald-Sun, Bernard Thomas, p. 14; © Thomas B. Shea/Getty Images, p. 15; © Giuseppe Cacace/Getty Images, p. 15 (inset); Luigi Chiesa/Wikimedia Commons (CC BY-SA 3.0), p. 16; © Joe Quinn/Alamy, p. 17; GH1/Adidas/ Newscom, p. 18; © Michael Krinke/Vetta/Getty Images, p. 19; © Laura Westlund/ Independent Picture Service, pp. 20, 22; © leungchopan/Bigstock.com, p. 21; © Tony French/Alamy, p. 23; © Russ Bishop/Alamy, p. 23 (inset); © Jonathan Kingston/National Geographic Image Collection/Alamy, p. 24; © Daniel Milchev/The Image Bank/Getty Images, p. 25; © iStockphoto.com/DOUGBERRY, p. 26; © iStockphoto.com/mbbirdy, p. 27; AP Photo/New Balance, p. 28.

Front cover: © iStock/Thinkstock.